THE KING

THE KING

Richie Phillips

Copyright © 2022 Richie Phillips

The moral right of the author has been asserted.

Apart from any fair dealing for the purposes of research or private study, or criticism or review, as permitted under the Copyright, Designs and Patents Act 1988, this publication may only be reproduced, stored or transmitted, in any form or by any means, with the prior permission in writing of the publishers, or in the case of reprographic reproduction in accordance with the terms of licences issued by the Copyright Licensing Agency. Enquiries concerning reproduction outside those terms should be sent to the publishers.

Matador
Unit E2 Airfield Business Park,
Harrison Road, Market Harborough,
Leicestershire. LE16 7UL
Tel: 0116 2792299
Email: books@troubador.co.uk
Web: www.troubador.co.uk/matador
Twitter: @matadorbooks

ISBN 978 1 8031 3048 4

British Library Cataloguing in Publication Data.
A catalogue record for this book is available from the British Library.

Printed and bound in Great Britain by 4edge Limited
Typeset in 11pt Minion Pro by Troubador Publishing Ltd, Leicester, UK

Matador is an imprint of Troubador Publishing Ltd

For Claire, with thanks for everything you do and everything you are.

Alabama

Open skies; heat sucking life,
Swirling up through circling buzzards, silently high,
Feeding the blue, unending blue.
Dark forest and deep creek
Terracotta tracks throwing up the rusty dust
Scattering the cardinals.
Trodden down beauty, and tales untold,
Shells of ghost cars,
Old Glory hanging lifeless.
Catfish and snapping turtle,
Tin castle ruins and empty casings.
Holding hands at Momma's table,
Prayers and cornbread;
Rolling Tide, a cold beer,
Songs on the porch and a peach evening sky.
Friends they have become
And Daughter that I love.

BARRIOS

Skipping, tipping and tapping,
Shrill staccato echoes
Within its spruce cloister.
Gently calling
A hovering dragonfly
Or a small painted bird.

Softly it swirls
Like cirrus in a summer sky,
Tricking through the olive groves;
Lullabies for the graves
Spills through the fields
Where the cane grows high.

The tired, weathered faces
Are smiling and warm
Their arms outstretched
"Salud y que aproveche"
He is a friend to them all.

Agustin Barrios (1895 - 1944)

Beyond the Divide

An arbitrary line, preserved in stone.
In tired clothes, slipped quietly out
At Friedrichstrasse and beyond the divide.
To monochrome landscape; cold, grey and flat.
Hypnotic similarity, easily confused.
Occasionally, a car. Cream or powder blue
Or yet more grey, in and upon grey
Smoke and rust.
Unremarkable shops, sparsely stocked
Waning choices, cheap cigarettes and whisky
Opium for the masses…
Back at U8, soldiers bristling with guns
Crackle of boot upon platform
Eyes everywhere, stoic and detached.
Shuffling aboard
Out of the darkness, brought back to light.
Even then the signs were there;
Colours bleeding.
Waters breaking.
Re-birth.

BERLIN 1988

Black Shadow

Kick, kick, kick over…
Gasps, splutters and hums.
I am Gagarin
Aiming for the stars.

Growling through the dappled lanes
Thundering, thrusting, pumping,
Punching holes in the air
Consummating fuel and fire.

O! Hammer of Thor
Outrun this evening's grasp
As dark shapes engulf the Earth
We fly

Pilots and pioneers
Were your fathers
Dreamers and grafters, mine.
You gave them hope;
Now I give you life.

Bridge of Sighs

In times of Mariners and Merchants,
Traders and troubadours,
Renaissance splendour, feast for the senses,
Pickings for the rich.

Deep beneath the lagoon
The lowly sleepers slumber in dark gloom,
Weight of the City, wailing in the water,
Heavy, engulfed and burdened.

In the cells, beneath the Doge's Palace
The lowly condemned suffer
In the filth, darkness and disease
Wrath of the City, woes of the World.

Crossing that bridge, window like a flower,
Last longing look at the lagoon,
A window on farewell.

Met up with my wife in The Florian
And over the 20 euro lattes
She said "so now you know".
I did. It never left me;
Neither beauty nor aching yearn,
Descending steps, never to return.

VENICE 2012

BRIEFLY SPEAKING..

Cries and sleeping
Talking and walking
Mummy and Daddy
Toys and books
Coat pegs and classrooms
Janet and John
Music and Movement
Val John and Pete
Look and Read
Seeing and Doing
Torment and Tag
Kiss chase and flares
Test tubes and tripods
Woodwork and Woolworths
Exchanges and Exams
Shakespeare and Lorca
Prediction and Perdition
Execution and Resurrection
Romance and Relocation
Sartre and Kierkegaard
Friends and NMEs
Graduation and London
Home and the Dole

Broke and a Girl
Job and Prospects
Trying and Saving
Betrayal and Behaviour
California and Virginia
Career and Colleagues
Friends and Lovers
Marriage and Rings
Husband and Wife
Routine and Holiday
Life and Death
Better and Worse
Son and Daughter
Mice and Wheels
Change and hard choices

Implosion and Impasse
Silence and Solitude
Widow and Window
Happiness and Colour
Care and Belief
Gardens and Cafes
Amsterdam and Venice
Forward and Positive
Unity and Understanding
World and Wine
Peers and Mentors
Trusted and Trusting
Changing and Challenges
Refresh and recycle
More life is found.

Car Lot

Resplendent, yet redundant;
Glaring or twinkling?
Promises billow in the breeze,
Easy ways,
All. Pockets. Received.

A man ambles between the columns
With wax and cloth
Bodies tormented by gull and crow:
White on blue
Blackcurrant dirty on silver.

Dusty tarmac bejeweled
By spittle of hose
The flags hang limp.
Holed up, thirty yards back
With lures all set,
Creator, curator, creature;
The animals are asleep.

Once they stormed the plains,
Once they paraded with pride;
Now like artefacts
Destinations unknown
Future never guaranteed.

Comfort and Joy?

Stretched, dry, faded, blunt
Energy low and sources few,
Waiting cold in dead of night
Back to zero, all we knew
Alone in National plight.

Bravely now, the coloured lights
Quelled their glow, remained on show
Smoldering in the fog
Headlight blinds, the lane unwinds
An old man walks his dog.

We wait – it is a time of waiting.
Hopes and fear, made real this year
Not young anticipation.
Choice we make, threats of mistake
Balancing a nation.

(CHRISTMAS 2020)

Corrida

Blood and sand; a flag created
In a nation's earth.
This febrile cauldron
Where the dust is burnished by blazing noon sun,
No shade here now, nowhere to run.

Crudely fashioned bleached stone seats
Heat strips peeling gloss on black burladero
Nowhere to hide today.

Last night the roar; the pounding cloven hoof.
Now, matador, your ancestors call,
And culture expects the best of deaths.

The tercio de muerte
Muleta taunts this noble animal,
They dance the tanda, to final steps
The estocada.

Handkerchiefs like fluttering doves,
But no peace here, until today.
Searching for the meaning
In the mad heat of mid-day.

(Plaza de Toros de Almeria)

CROW

Ripping through the gentle dawn,
Blood throated curse scolds the new day,
Perched atop the withered oak,
Jurassic grip on dead white bark
He waits…

Floating through the misty field
The assassin.

Dancing on a stony altar
Flaps at cars, returns,
Pecks and pulls the entrails
Of the twisted kill.

Nesting o'er the larch and poplar
In his kingdom
Too close to God.

Floating through the misty fields
The assassin.

Sight fixed, await the twitch.

Curtis

Out of the mills and machinery;
Borne of Blake and Bowie,
Found the spirit, found the feeling
In epileptic ectoplasm
He told the tale of Now.
Deeper, harder, true
Inward. Anxiety. Never
Curtailed.
Permanent.

Ian Curtis (Joy Division, 1956-1980)

Daydreaming

A hot August afternoon,
Staring out into the green open
At two batsmen,
In a drinks interval.

In his dusty baggy green cap
Trademark white kerchief
Rose faced and silver brow
"Keep going champ, not much batting to come
The quicks will be back, you'll prefer it coming on."

"The guy this end" I say
"Gets the odd one to rip,
But length's very full,
Get your foot down, plenty of ones and two's
In front of point."

Next ball short, foot moves back
Eye on ball, and wait, wait, crack
No one here is stopping that
Fifty up, and raise my bat.
Down he comes, "well batted champ"
Lovely square cut, practiced those enough."

Then, a slow drifter
Grabs the dirt and spins,
Entices the old fighter,
Thinnest edge of thins.

He doesn't wait, turns on his heels
Towards the pavilion,
Beyond the green,
Beyond this Earth,
Onwards, up into the blue,
And out of mortal view.
He has gone.

And I am in my garden half asleep
We lived for days like these.
Memories are all we have.
Preserved for us by the "kind old sun"
Forever he remains not out.

ALAN "ALY" PHILLIPS (1937-2017)

Drake

Handsome prince
In a lonely room
Tools of the trade his only friends
Guitar, tea, cigs and pills
Turning the keys, inventing new keys
New chords and new heights

Shy, quiet and beautiful
Music and the Man
River, city, field and wood
Flute and cello brushing colour
Into his monochrome world.

Loved by many, known by none
Too shy to shine his light.
Frightened by a black dog?
Slipped away one night.

Heavy soul rose up so high
Shone for all to see
Touching all of those who seek
A special "place to be".

Nick Drake (1948-1974)

Dubrovnik

Merchants and warriors,
The Old Town;
High up on the rampart,
Looking back over centuries
Across red rooftops and sapphire seas.

Within foreboding walls,
Epic gothic structure
And Baroque majesty,
Cobbled streets, old trades and new,
Artists and performers.
Sometimes the mighty sea
Will give up its treasure.

The pearl, still coveted
Twentieth century siege
Seven months of raining Hell,
Shell and mortar blast.
Old Town protected
Aggressor abated
New identity, new beginning.

Invasion now of different kind
Mecca for TV fantasists
Lovers of art and architecture
Happy hosts and grateful guests,
Posebno mjesto.

Equinox

I sat and watched their "V" formation
Flying straight and true,
Southbound, unerring,
In the cloudless blue.
Tiny specks, like grains
Of sands,
Of time.

How will it be
When they return?
What will have changed?
What will we learn?

The following night,
Skies ashen grey;
The geese were right.
Shorter grows the day, longer the night.

Tired faces, empty gazes,
Looking where they flew;
Horizon white,
Blank pages.
Blank ages
Could turn either way.

Expiry Date

Scorched earth and white shadows,
The Overture
To End of Days.
Point of no return?

Flawed design, haemorrhaged death;
A rusted theme park
Where Ghost Trains linger

Missing letter tiles
On a church sign, in Nazareth, Pennsylvania
Broken Jesus, whilst TV priests prosper.
Volunteers where so many babies cry;
Empty the eyes, emaciated frames,
Hunger fed by lies.

It starts with love.
With kind words and care.
There is no cost,
But it's a long way there.

The smallest steps mark new beginning
From the Revelation,
Behold Genesis.

For a Friend

Remember as a child, you rode the carousel
And every time around, a wave to mum and dad?
Those fleeting glimpses are now all he has,
Snatches of reality, occasional glances
Of familiarity; but it is still him.

Don't try to understand – there is no logic
Where he now lives, acquiescence is the key
And gentle persuasion.

Slowly, painfully turning in, towards himself
Bowing, bending
To an embryonic final form.

You will have long since cried all your tears
And there will be a peace once again
And a quiet gratitude that he is now free.

GILMOUR

Endearing images;
Young, long-haired, handsome,
Echoes around Pompeii
And the old burly grey fox
At home in the Park.

Enduring craft;
Timeless pieces,
Swiss watch precision,
Aural audio perfection.

Riffs run, ring and resonate,
High fidelity, high functioning,
Voice squeezes through.
Faint fuzz, damp, kick, bend;
Tricks of the trade
Black, the instrument,
Myriad colours, its art.

Erudite and eloquent,
Esteemed and elegant,
In Rock's heraldry, his flag unfurled.

David Gilmour (Pink Floyd)

Grief

The grass is trimmed
Edges neatly skimmed.
Stones stand awkwardly, like embarrassed onlookers
Leaning this way and that;
Some have crumbled, some lie flat.
Names hidden to all but a few.
And to the south, near four o'clock
There is a block
A small, chipped block
Childlike chiseled
A sad and solitary "K".
Committed to the dirty water;
Hymn of the Cherubim.

(KEITH PHILLIPS 1945-51)

Hedging (on the Armistice)

The brittle latticed twigs
Spitting shards, somersaulting in gunmetal sky
Gold, green and brown.
Ruptured wood, crackling.
Scattered birds, cackling.

Flailing arms and legs
Shells raining in anthracite sky
Spitting shrapnel, sitting ducks
Greens and greys, red and brown
Shattered youthful dreams,
Scattered fire, gargling life.

The trees undressed
Disheveled land,
Miracles hidden underground
Mother Nature's secret shift.
Whilst here above, the Peace returns
This inverted resurrection,
The circle begins again.

Her Majesty's Pleasure

Filing down the corridor
Anonymous, amorphous,
Dressed in grey;
Tattoos, scars and crucifixes;
Shaven heads
Beards and dreads
Stale and pallid.

Frowning gazes
Enemy on another wing;
A pointed finger
Angry gesture and under-breath curses
Before they're moved away.

Some try hard,
Others, by duress, are bored.
Gazing out of windows
Yearning for the sun.

Discussion always best
Summary notes to end

Treat them just like someone
Take them somewhere else
And they have questions.

Relief palpable,
Back through the metal doors
"Cheers guv" they bid farewell
Shut in? Shut out?

Abject misery, stark institution,
Caged or lost souls,
What did they do?
Sometimes volunteered, never asked.
There but for the grace of God, we go.

Hikikomori

In tiny bedrooms
Crowded space
At octogenarian behest,
Withdrawn, reclusive
Generation.

No heirs apparent
Simple empty lives
Serving those protected;
Ashamed and belittled
Denied space to grow
No blossom in the dark.

Robots and technology
No blood on hands
Knife, without honour
Through aching hearts
That knew no love.
Unconsummated, barren
Forty years stillborn.

"Him"

―※―

Within a minute, it had gone.

"I saw something," said Ben the Barman
"Over the stadium, behind the East Stand."

"Probably the Army base", dismissed Paul the Postman.
"All the cool stuff happens under the cover of darkness".

"I saw it too," laughed Vanessa the Vet,
"I told you UFOs were real."
Stranger truths.

By Boxing Night, we'd passed it off.
Lost amid the copious drinks
TV Schedules and broken toys,
Nudging out the adhesive relatives.
Arguments over Scrabble
And the favourite, falling at the last.
We all moved on.

No one was ready then.
They remained unwilling, to let him in.
The miracles dismissed as magic,

The words, as heresy.
Ostracised, he wondered
Finding no peace;
The stars all went out
And we remained
Together, quite alone.

HITTING THE BUFFERS

"The train wreck arriving at Platform Ten
Is the delayed fifty something from Guildford.
Terminating here.
We apologise for the late arrival of this service…"

It was a beautiful morning
Sun set cornflakes aglow,
Kiss from the wife and a coffee to go.

But, heaving platform, standing room only
Irritating ear-bud hiss.
Open mouthed chewing, body odour, bicycles,
Anonymous farting
And billowing bags,
Faltering progress.
Grinding to a halt.

Only delaying the daily inevitable
Only the names had changed
Budgets, forecasts, huddles and
Competitive Junior Managers,
Loathsome little shits.

Looked up at the skyline, beyond Waterloo;
A plane took flight to warmer climes
Removed his coat, it was his time.
Sent a message, phone in the Thames,
Mulberry briefcase, thrown in the Thames
Hackett umbrella, similar fate,
And no fucks given that he was late.
Tie discarded, a patisserie;
Early retirement, finally free.

Items

Millions of items;
Educational, recreational
Vital, or disposable.
All purchased,
Most, wanted.

Automation and algorithms
Temporary their harmony
With Human hands
Digging for victory.
Come into the Factory
Make it work;
The robots need you.

The wheels are rolling
Millions of items
Are moving
Thousands of miles,
And I am still here

In a hole
Where the Sun never shines
And myriad screens flash;

Weary the metal clunks
And the motors whine
And the belts rattle
And the beat goes on…

Go to, or home from,
Always in the dark,
Waiting for the Sun.

KUBRICK

Just what do you think you're doing?
Massacres and masquerades
Often slowly making and breaking
Of Man. Of men.

Belittling and beguiling
Nobles and nudity
Twins in the corridor
Monoliths and monkeys
Forbidden love and worlds within worlds.

Gunnery sergeants, animals, cowards
Cheats who prosper,
Slavery and opportunity
Ultraviolence, intergalactic.

Full catalogue
Dark web of life
Deranged, debased
Defiled and detailed
Turning in on ourselves.

He's outside
He's beyond
In over their heads.
Get some!
I'm Spartacus.

I'm afraid…

Legacies

You left a hole,
You left a mess;
What did it all mean?
We had to guess.

Best china and christening spoons,
Scribbled drafts, was this a book?
Recorded programmes, rows of knitting,
Remind how short a time it took.

Purchased cards for special days
Flower tubs, heads hung, bereft;
Voicemail messages not erased,
Only threads of living left.

Frozen in this strangest time,
Feeling the exposure;
Waiting to move safely on,
Still not near to closure.

Letting It Be

(The demise of The Beatles)

Something in the way they moved,
Suggested paths of no return.
The orchestrator dead; engineer did what he could,
Flashes of brilliance, stretches of moderate.

Hallucinogens and altered states.
The small note that said "yes"
Became significant other, more duo than fifth.
Reports of death, kingmakers, subterfuge,
All juice squeezed out, running on empty;
Short tempers and long winding roads.
Out on the roof, one last hurrah.

Tape flicks empty spool
Backing into four corners
I'm losing you
Called for a Priest
Father Mackenzie wiped his hands.

Loki's Gift

In fading light
Sun's dying breath
One final kiss, ignites
Dry tinder in chorus;
Opening sequence
Of this, your requiem
This quiet parade.

Ancient nature feeding flame
Wood, coal and peat
First percussive crackle;
Furious now the melody
Fortissimo
Under Odin's spell
Flames and Thor's hammer
Dancing syncopation.

Somewhere, in the pyre of Olaf's floating tomb
A spirit is born.
Bequeathed to sons on Isles remote
And onwards, outwards, reaching down
Eight hundred years,
Warm the glow.

Lost Property

Somewhere in a large drawer
Amid watches and wallets, umbrellas and rings,
Forgotten purchases pristine in plastic wrapping,
Somewhere between brooches, compacts,
Good pens and spectacle abrasion,
Somewhere down between pinching metal and leather
Mobile devices and homesick toys
Are thoughts, are prayers, feelings, souls,
Purposes and energies lie the same with betrayed love
And unfulfilled wishes.

We took them with us on our journeys
But, left, lost or just discarded,
Did not arrive.

Manson

In isolation.
Subjugated, emasculated,
Locked him up, shut us all in
…And set him free.
Because, he said,
We're all in our own prisons
And we are all
Our own Wardens.

A little man, black eyes;
Career criminal.
At best, coward
At worst, Antichrist
Or your worst acid trip.
Sometimes psychotic,
Occasionally lucid,
Intrigued, we too become his captives.

"They weren't born that way,
Someone put it on them."
From nothing, of nothing
Mills still silent after war.
Insisted did no wrong,
Yet ordered the chaos,
World of pain; numbers and colours.

And the snake will perform
For the money they'd thrown
And the churches you bought
Became overgrown.
At the end of the line.

Helter Skelter
Pigs, in blood.
Rise! On his command
The final embers hissed,
A generation perished;
Cielo to Altamont,
Death of the beautiful,
End of the dream.

Mostar

Three years under siege
In a crude basement room
No news of home, no way out
Said at times he found it hard to breathe.
Not from gun smoke, nor dust from shells
Nor from the crumbling monuments
But through a pure and simple
Fear.

A radio, and a daily running of the sniper's gauntlet.
Euro Rock Stations, Winds of Change,
Brothers in Arms, fathers at home,
Broken dreams of a team in blue
And a green eyed girl, he once knew.

Even twenty years on, it felt betrayed by time
Bullet pock-marked walls, mortar ravaged streets
Still played an empty requiem, ringing silently round
The mountains and the hills.
But amid the broken aftermath
Behold ! A white stone bridge
Created in its former image, piece by piece, in Peace
By brave new friends, together born again.

He remained, re-built, and raised a family.
Told the history, taught with love,
No longer in fear of the former
Knowing the latter, will always prevail.

(MOSTAR, BOSNIA – HERZEGOVINA, 2017)

Nocturne

 ⚜

Warm glow in cool darkness
Books lean, tiredly,
Cushions slump,
Portraits bow in shadows
Gently caressed keys,
Notes dropped as if some magic trail,
Blanket of stars
Songs of the Night.
Time to breathe, to heal,
Bathing in each moonlit chord,
Languishing in the lapping tide.
Subtle changing hues
Of purple, crimson, indigo,
Colours of the night.
Cognac's auburn swell
Quiet, sweet and sensual burn.
Gazing with warm pride
At sepia tarnished frame
Three ranks, one seated
He stands with peaked cap,
Peaceful and assured
Amid all the chaos.
Nothing can touch him.

He seems to know
It plays for him.
Guardian of our night.

Percy Keevil (Royal Flying Corps 1914-18)

Off the grid

Hear the whispering brook
The mountain breeze
And bird song
Flowing over the pebbled shallows,
Clear and certain.
See the eagle soaring
Deer, beaver and bear
Cold blue and grey
Warm green and brown.

Peace I bought, not with Army pension
But with my youth
My best years,
My brothers in arms,
The blood spilled,
The people I killed
Drugs to sleep, to cope, to be
The heavy price I paid, was me.

Old trapper's hut;
Simple means, metal, wood
Off the track, out of range
Booby trapped, tightly wrapped,

Tied down, tied up,
Notes, knives, ropes,
Guns and skins,
Hard wired; one eye open.

Everything had changed
And no-one cared
Couldn't fit, couldn't cope
After all was seen and done
Dead inside, withdrew.
Solitude, the lowest hand
Dealt blind by the World
Making sense of surviving.

See this peace? It's all I have,
I can't go home.
Sometimes I don't sleep
Sometimes I cry.
Months run into years;
It matters not
Where nothing ends.

On my Hundredth Birthday

A middle aged man sits down
And takes the time to hear
The things that he would wish himself
Upon his hundredth year.

"I wish you hope each January, life renewed in Year,
I wish you love in February, from all those you hold dear,
In March may daffodils all bloom to brighten your surrounds,
April showers and cuckoo May, all Spring's orchestral sounds.
Long warm evenings in June when days roll idly by
Wimbledon and Test Match, to occupy July.
Holidays in August, great-grandchildren on the beach,
Long walks in September with blackberries in reach,
See October landscape, with Turners on each path
And Elgar in November, around the Cenotaph,
Fine brandy in December, to warm with Christmas cheer,
And raise a glass to welcome
Many future happy years.

Reinvention

You would not invite
Friends to your house
With building work in progress
Neither comfortable nor safe.
But, when working on your self
They must all still come in
And walk through your life
With bare walls exposed
And shit everywhere.
We're works in progress
Don't look, don't judge,
It is transformation
Towards eventual renovation.

Rhine

Artery of Europe;
From flat nether lands
Through industrial outposts
And beauteous gorge,
With castles chiseled
And sprinkled with vine
And vivid, viridescent forests
To cities, ablaze with
Music, culture, commerce
Courtesy and conviviality.
Structures, stark, gothic
And Romanesque romance.
Chocolate box cafes.
All voices of a chorus
Reciting their anthems
With pride.

Saying Goodbye

Sun weighed down in the sky;
The shadows stretching
Foreboding science settling.
The World still turns, yet we are done.
Clutching at positives,
Something to build on, or cling to
In the empty days to come,
And speak of happy reunion,
Without the comfort of how, or when.
The early parted seconds,
Each one like an hour;
The days will fill themselves, eventually.
And with time, numb, desensitized
We find a setting
On which we can function;
Pieces shut down,
Attachments broken off,
Heart torn out
Stuffed back in,
Running on vapours,
But running……

Tank

Garden Centre; Hell on Earth.
Dithering old people, bored kids run feral
Masks to hide the sighs.
Seeking refuge, aquarium section.
Cool, quiet and dark – try to look interested…

Tank.
A television on their world.
Silvery minnows, shifting shoals
Larger specimens in gold,
Black and white.
And one looking out
At me.

Is me?
Shut in static, repetitive torment,
Not like the others.
Castle ruin, seaweed wreck
In and out, round and round,
Memory gone,
Day after day.

And then one that floats up
Attendants quick to act
Can't have image damaged
Murder after the fact.

The Artist

He was my cousin;
Straggled hair under tired fedora,
Unkempt unruly beard,
Stooping gait in quickstep, always carrying bags
"Hey man"…..

Nestling quietly on the wharf,
He sat and wove his spell.
Pastel, oil or watercolour,
Each a song in its own style.

With Lambert and with Butler
He puffed and fed his craft
Pulling in the elements, filling up the emptiness.
Tilting head inquisitive,
As would, as was, a small child,
Gentle the conductor and sweet his symphony
Of tone, of hue, of light and shade.

All the time, distracted, spoke of football, music, films,
Tin cups from a shopping bag, filled by the flask in old tweed coat.
"Did you see the game last night?

Are Mum and Dad OK?
I bought that book on Lennon…
In town the other day…"

Kept an awful lot of things
And gave much work away
He was off the chart
And out of a job
Above the clouds, and
Heading up the wall.
Not really of, or for this World.
No real ambition nor grand vision,
But saw it all so clearly.

Captured and recreated
Those things normal men
Could never express,
Like light, like air, like earth, like fire and water
It wasn't meant for him,
But he knew all of them.

Even the sweetest wine, in time
Turns to bitter vinegar,

And anxious, agitated, alone
The Old Master called him Home.

But this, the very best of men
Bequeathed us all
His multi layered and multicoloured
Legacy.

Gregory D. Phillips (1952 – 2011)

The Nurse

Tall, yet somehow taller still
In hat and cape
Flat shoes fleetly flitting over floors
Polished, sterile sheen,
Strong stone pillars
And she is here.

In fonder times
Of newsreel, smaller cars
And bedside manner;
Three channels, reduced power
Experience over intelligence,
Steadfast and unwavering
She was there.

Old values and new worlds
Knit together like craft
Lucid, alert, patient, scholarly;
When all but the strongest
Threw in their bloodstained towels,
She remained.
Front of the house
At work in theatre,

Or prompting life quietly
From the wings:
Lead the line with regard,
With humour and aplomb.
And when her work was done
Cast away her cape
Grew wings
She was here

(Nancie Phillips 1932-2021)

The Trawlermen

Sometimes, as if a Leviathan
The merciless sea
Would raise itself and smash
These weathered hulls.

Others, gentle pulsing still,
Feeling for the deep.
Always different, and the same.
The old hands know before truth reveals
Some days plenty, and plenty, none.

What hope for tomorrow?
Says the trawlerman
The salesman, the farmer, the shopkeeper, busker,
The soldier, dug in deep.

Low glow the harbour lights,
Mist reveals the day;
Again, we revolve.

"Torch Song"

Blue-tinged dusky mist
Sad trumpet spirals and sprawls
Across the empty floor,
The muffled brushes lead an aching piano
In the final dance tonight.

Bass vibration, through table and through glass
Stirs the final slug
Snare whispers time to go.

A smattering ripple of pattering hands
She bows and slips back
Into the night
And leaves our untold love
On its perpetual precipice.

Transition

Leaves wet, cold, limp
Hanging precariously to sodden branches
Barely holding on
Gold and russet, each a different tale,
No two the same,
Gentle release, and final dance.

And in a quiet room
All branches now removed
Short, shallow breaths
Prepares for autumnal departure.

Uncle Neddy

Standing on the bridge
Bitter chill creeps down
The Blackwater
Down the centuries,
Heavy clouds stirred,
Spitting with icy rain
We reached the house.

Simple rooms above the shop,
Peat fire, piles of books;
A Nun made tea
His best china.
And the man himself
Almost blind, stretched out
Gnarled, arthritic hands
Smiled and squeezed mine,
Voice a frail, high whisper
Strained to hear, spoken slowly.

One hundred years.
Seen it all.
Hardship, hunger
Rising, reconciling and rebirth
Old countries and new lands
Portents, purgatory and peace.
Told his tale.
Hour of gold,
Majestic narrative,
The magic, and purpose of age,
To History entrusted.

COUNTY CORK – 1993

Weeds

A gentle reminder
From Mother Earth;
Where we thought
Nothing could survive
Behold, the weed
And its ugly flourish.

A story of hope
Of triumph in adversity
Irresistible life force
Driving through
All obstructions
All inanimate objects.

When all is lost
The weed prevails;
Obeys no order
Requires no help.
Stretching for the sun,
Because it can.

West Virginia

One billion stars;
They felt so close
Yet out of reach.
How small and insignificant we must have seemed
To anyone or anything
Looking back at us..

How could silence feel so loud?
This the only time that life stood still.
Nothing mattered from the past,
Nothing known which lay ahead.
It was our time, our special place, in Time.

The same stars all ages viewed,
Princes, prophets, presidents
In their respective reigns,
Soldiers, slaves and sons of God
In their inflicted pains
We looked out at Forever
Standing at the start
A billion stars to light the way
An eternity apart.

Where Love Grows

It matters very little, in what you may believe
We all reflect in different ways, when comes our time to grieve.
A sparkle on the water, a ladder to the sky,
An echo in a quiet lane, a teardrop in your eye.
The love you gave to all of us, became a mighty seed,
Tended by our fond regard, it grows, and lives to feed.
Where love grows, then hope can thrive,
And strength to carry on,
And quietly, gently, in this way
You never will be gone.

(Carole Phillips. 1942-2020)

WHISPERING DEATH

Ambling back, with a loose-limbed lethargy
To his mark.
Final polish, turns and bows.
Begins.

Gathering speed
Body grows erect
Floating over the scorched turf
Now in full rhythmic flow.

Final stride, leaps, arching back
And, in fluid motion,
Propels.

Fizzing like a tracer bullet
Instrument of death
Catapults from concrete earth
Shattered ash clatters.

Cacophony of cans, cornucopia
Of horns, drums and cheers
Like some sacrifice,
The Gods approve.

MICHAEL HOLDING (WEST INDIES CRICKETER)

"X"

Twelve to a room,
Dark chimneys, flooded gullies,
Scorched fields,
Built all with bare hands
And rude implement.
Or in the Poor House
Or asylums;
Filth and squalor
Disease and early death,
Cold sunrise to aching sunset,
All marked,
With an "X".

Revealed to me,
Names and their pains,
Census or certificate,
"Pauper"
"Idiot"
"Died aged 4"
Labourers, Mariners
Carters and Cleaners
Sweeps and Scullery Maids
Runaway sailors and

Bastard sons.
All marked
With an "X".

And what lines that famine
Plague and fire
Could not eradicate
Wars did.
Conscripted,
Lions led by donkeys
Fields of France
White anonymous stones
Untitled and not entitled
Even with an "X"

What "privilege"?
What apology required
From those
Marked with an "X"?

Zero

Up on the Moor
Curly, unruly mop
Flailing in the half-light wind
What's he doing up there?

He says he's recording silence.
At least he was…
"Now I'm recording you lot
Asking me what I am doing…"

Now he's conducting feedback
As speaker levels wince and glow
In a manufactured chill;
"I'm warming them up…
But drums sound better in the lift
So you're in there, Steve…"

He has stopped the take,
Had a fag and smashed a glass
Put sound through the Synare.
Now he's hiding under the desk,
Because he's bored and won't share his sweets .

"Bollocks" he says (to no-one in particular)
Claims it sounds like everything else done
In the last 20,000 years….
"Turn that down, make it more 'yellow'
Do it more slowly but faster."
Adds some of this and then that
Takes it out, shakes it all about.

"I'm innovating",
Making notes in a shopping trolley,
Looking for his cough mixture
"Piss off….oh…
Got any booze?"
A few more arguments, the bottle is empty.
And it is done.

Oh…my ..God
It's beautiful
Like a painting that speaks to you
Light from blindness
Ethereal, eternal.

MARTIN HANNETT 1948-1991
PRODUCER, FACTORY RECORDS.

"THE KING"

The King (1)

A wooded lane
In English vale,
Lurcher lumbers beside
This quiet man.
Thin and early grey
Upright, moving lightly
Casts a long evening shadow.

The trees have started turning
Amber, crimson, gold,
The World rotates again.
Dim light from secluded haven
Over brook and under oak
Retaining stories, still.

They say he is a Doctor
But no practice here?
Someone did some homework
Confirming PhD – Balliol no less.
"Perhaps he is a specialist"
Was the publican's best guess.

He looked across the valley
Four counties wide
A photo from his wallet
Kissed then placed inside.

A gentleman, polite and gracious,
Living on his own
Philanthropist, from distance,
Neither church nor function
So no-one minded
After all, this is England.
But this is England…

The King (2)

Some forty years before;
A country at a time
Of great unrest.
Whispered mistrust
Flames fuelled by tales
Of illegitimate legacies.

A military coup, a new regime
A bloody revolution,
General hailed a great new dawn
And wealth redistribution.

The royal family, all slain,
Palace stormed and pillaged;
Burning flags, dancing hordes
Car horns and carbines.
The old order had fallen.

Yet the Old King was wise;
He felt the winds of change
Knew exactly what to do
To preserve his lineage.

And as the time came near
He took his only son,
Dressed him in rags
Baptised in mud and sand
Rolled inside a carpet
Driven out in tradesman's van.

The King had made arrangements
Moved precious pieces into play;
Income for another life
Many miles away.
Met by agents as agreed
Handed over, flown away
To England's safety
Assumed new name under the watch
Of a very secret service.

THE KING (3)

The Reverend Peter Young
And his wife Louise
Shepherds, foster parents,
Fully vetted, briefed and kind
Opened house and home
To the "orphaned refugee"
A multi-faith Borough,
Perfect disguise.

Compassion and instruction
Equals construction
Of another life and new name;
Eventually, his jigsaw story
Became distorted faithfully.

"There was a fire..
I was very young, but I remember
My father rolled me into a carpet
Wet with mud to protect me,
Gave me to someone
Who carried me through the fire, and away.
I felt the heat, heard the flames
And the screaming…

..the screaming.
Closed my eyes and ears
Fell asleep
And when I woke up far away
They told me
All my family had died"..

The Reverend Peter Young
And his wife Louise
And British Intelligence
Became the custodians
Of his Majesty
John.

The King (4)

When the time at last was right,
It was all explained.
The best people
Delivering chronology
The context and consequences;
The heaviest of crowns
Great as any cross.

Counsel for the young man
Who stoically, regally
Swallowed his grief,
Only betrayed by a quiet
But glistening tear.

Of all the provision made,
A single photograph,
Father, mother, sisters
Was all that mattered.

Difficult the days
Long the nights;
Studying came easily,
Fired by burning sense

Of duty to his Father
The King
Who had given up every thing
Except him.

All lives reduce
To simple questions;
Mere seconds in their asking
Generations in their answer
Forgive? Forsake? Revenge or Reinvention?

THE KING (5)

"An outstanding student
With an incisive, clinical mind,"
Somewhat reserved,
But gentle and kind.
John worked hard
On and around his subjects
Bringing ideas and suggestions
For new grounds and methods.

Away from campus
The struggle grew harder;
There is a seed
In all of us
That seeks to know
It's own true place.

History is a beguiling mistress,
And forensic examination
Of all empires
Reveals a pageant of death
Banners soaked in blood;
Corruption, conspiracy
And the shortcomings of men.

It had not always been
A loyal and loving family;
Proud and benevolent
Craft of his father
Yet, bloodlines traced back
To war and famines
It took generations
For the snakes' eggs to hatch
But hatch they did.

And since the coup
Chaos, murder and poverty
Guerillas and insurgency,
Wealth redistribution
Into one and several hands
Of lascivious generals,
To oppress the people
By the machete and gun
No cause, but their own.

Much harder then,
Than any chemical equation
Or complex dissertation
A nation in pain.
Powerless,
Nails in a cross.
This Revelation.

The Reverend Peter Young
And his wife Louise
Confronted one visit
"Where was your God ?"

"Your father's actions....
Not that you should seek revenge
But be left free to live
A free and proud man
To do good, to love, to be loved.
These, your father's actions
Were those of a man
Following his Deity
My "God", his, and yours too."

The King (6)

Purchased from an old Estate
A huntsman's Lodge
Gated, updated,
Obscure and secure.

No wish to stand out, no ostentation,
But an earnest wish
To honour his family.

Articles for *The Lancet*
Under nom de plume
Shrewd investor, vinyl collector
Remembering happy times.

Best of all
A vintage motorcycle.
Anonymity and freedom,
The open roads,
Uphill and down dale
Butterfly heart
In flight he found true freedom.

And though he was not short
Of friends and loose associations
From weekly visits to local pub
And village celebrations,
He dared not to look for love
In such intimate locations.

Instead, escort girls from the City
High-end business
Asked no questions
Offered everything at a price
Did everything for a price
Fulfilled nothing.

It was a Sunday afternoon,
At a small lakeside café
Appeared another machine
He looked up and nodded
Lifting helmet revealed
A woman
"Hello" she smiled.
"I always wanted one like yours
But this was all I could afford.."

"Temperamental things" he smiled
"But that's part of the fun,
Would you like to join me
For a cup of tea and a bun?"

THE KING (7)

"I'm Polly".

She was a radiologist,
An Army widow;
Wed only seven months
Husband on his final tour
Stood on an IED
Somewhere near Boboji,
Both destroyed by War.

Slowly, she rebuilt her life
With courage, dignity and respect,
Exploring now new avenues
No children to protect.

He listened, heard no other sound
Amid the lunchtime cups
Rattling cutlery or coughing machines
A voice as soft as rain
Whispering on parched earth
Ten minutes?
Like the blink of an eye

"Enough about me…
What about you?"

This time his oft-rehearsed
Cobbled back-story
Seemed harder to tell.
Scrambled to the medical link
But safer than he knew.

"How terrible" she lamented
"But how proud
Your parents would be"
The hook was in;
He smiled at her
"Would you care for more tea?"

And she was beautiful;
So alive, attentive, fun
Intelligent and adventurous,
Something more than fate.

Agreed before they went
Their separate ways,
To meet again.
And when they did
She suggested dinner
A more traditional date
Her choice, his pleasure.

Sitting in the Huntsman's Lodge
Internal questions started;
Like finger marks on lenses
Microscopic fears and doubts
Dismantling defences.

The King (8)

At a cosy corner table
Of a smart boutique hotel
They sat.

Polly's radiance cast
An aura, brighter than a thousand suns
Speaking, laughing
Completely natural, unaware.
Uncomplicated company
He was immersed.

A moonlit walk,
And a first kiss, again
Adolescent butterflies
Spread kaleidoscope wings
Rorschach images
Suggestive, clear.

Planned before parting
For several weeks hence
A weekend at the Huntsman's Lodge

Driving home, a foetal thought.
The right thing to do?
Torn between
Honouring that which he once loved
And that which he
Was growing to love.

Brief the joy,
Longer the torment.
Then came the reminder.
This was England.

THE KING (9)

It so happened,
The 40th Anniversary
Of the coup approached.

A news channel producer
Formed the idea;
A documentary
Marking the occasion;
Deemed to be an item
Of public and global interest.

And so, it came to pass
The programme aired,
Laden with depressing details
Of poverty, corruption
Oppression and fear
A once proud kingdom
Now a Non-Party State.

And in presenting the history,
A copy of that same family photograph
As the one in his wallet.
Description of what befell
No sordid detail spared.
And ending the segment
With a Judas kiss
"The body of the Prince
Was never found."

Kathy Ridley
Paused the screen.

The King (10)

At number 2, Granary Lane,
Lived Dave and Kathy Ridley,
Villagers of thirty years
Family firm and volunteers
In the Village Shop.

Steady, unremarkable
Took on the antiques business
When Kathy's father died.
Dave's determination held
Where others might subside.

Kathy somewhat spoiled,
Ideas above her station;
Dave kept busy
She kept her looks
Enjoyed parties and flirtation.

Fascinated by the mystery man
Ever since his arrival
Always mentioned him to Dave
Who'd joke "I have a rival !"
Polite but always distanced,

John managed the rapport
But Kathy felt attraction
And somehow longed for more.

Dreamed on empty wet shop days
Of a wild and torrid affair
A silly, secret construct
Of too much time to spare.
Put her time to better use
Researched her family tree
New consuming interest
Was found in History.

Truth, stranger than fiction,
"Agreed", she said "that's right"
But nothing would prepare her
For what would come that night.

Kathy Ridley
Paused the screen.

"The body of the Prince
Was never found…"

Looked at the "still"
More closely now
Kept 'hold' feature on
"Dave, just come and look at this
Does he not look like John ?..."

The King (II)

Dave Ridley remained sceptical,
"It's forty years ago,
Could be anyone.."
Kathy Ridley, more insistent
"He's always been a mystery
And the timing is spot on."

" A quiet village, out of the way
It all seems rather odd
Living out there on his own,
In that hunting lodge.."

"Your mind is over-active"
Dave dismissively sighed
There's better things for you to do,
That cannot be denied.
If you put all that energy
Into the plan we wrote
Our business would be thriving
Not fighting to stay afloat".

"And what is that supposed to mean ?"
She angrily replied.

"Look at this.."
A balance sheet
Which told a tale of debt
"We could even lose this house
It's been our worst year yet.
No-one wants it any more
The reason we're in hock
Too much out in overheads and storing too much stock."

Dave, defeated, went to bed,
Kathy blinded (but not myopic)
Pushed the button back to 'play'
Returned to former topic.
Saw the people struggling
And war crimes not indicted
"The country badly needs a King…

..Could they be reunited?

And if I did this wondrous thing
It would surely be rewarding
I'll find out the producer's name
At the end of the recording.

..Or maybe the papers? "…

THE KING (12)

Money changes people.

Kathy Ridley viewed it as
A parachute, arresting a fall,
And sought affirmation
From her own circle
But only a choice few;
Ownership was everything.

Meanwhile, moving quietly
About his own business
John completed some research
Co-wrote a reference book
And took a few days
To walk the hills;
Time to think.

Evening calls to Polly
Feelings stronger by the day
Both ways.

At first he felt a strange regret,
But on close reflection,
He would thank
Those watching over..

And maybe, if we believe
The voices from our past
This was destiny
Making early intervention.

"Polly, when we see each other,
I've something I must confess
It's not bad, not evil, not wrong,
Important, nonetheless…"

Polly pondered, taken aback,
But goodness kept her strong
Told him she'd be ready
Wouldn't have to wait too long.

Driving home, fighting inside
Did he need to say this now?
But to have a future with her
She'd have to know, somehow.

Mentally tired,
The welcoming lights of home
He sighed with relief
Pulled car to halt,
Window down to enter code

One shot, one flash
The Money shot.
Direct hit.

The King (13)

"Mr Galbraith, I have a problem."

The call he hoped
Would never have to be made.

Galbraith, calm and measured,
"Yes sir, I agree.
Can you leave discreetly
Is there somewhere you can be –
To buy ourselves a little time?"
And Polly said "to me".

Mick the farmer from next door
Appeared within the hour
"John, someone was creeping round..
I think it was the Press;
Rumours of a long-lost King
I don't know the rest."

And so it was
Mick became the first to know.

"I did hear rumours in the pub,
Looks like your cover's blown.
I'll keep the dog here on the farm
You'll have to come alone."
A Land Rover across the fields
Laying in the back
Underneath a tarp, like years before

Magic priest hole single track
Service road to Motorway
How could life repeat this way ?

"Climb up here now, in the front
Keep your cap and glasses on
We're on the motorway at last
Where d'you want to go now, John ?"

The King (14)

"We may not have much time",
Said Galbraith over phone
"My guess is that the photo
Is the final piece in play.
I fully expect it to appear
Across the Media today.

So, sit tight, sir
Stay now where you are;
We'll sit down and devise a plan
I'll come to you, by car.

In the meantime sir, please give some thought
To your response.
I appreciate the difficult factors here,
We will help you
Whatever you decide to do."

Finally the solace
Of Polly's lounge cum office
"What's this all about?"

It took several hours
Tea, toast and tears
And Polly felt a pain she had
Forgotten over years
A tender pain
A man in turmoil
Fighting to be strong
Wondering if, in her heart
Was where he might belong.

The following day
A startled man
Through the window of a car
Omnipresent in the Press;
From
"Heir he is", to
"The Man who may be King"
"Local Doctor is a Prince"
"Royal Arrival".
TV dishes, vans and staff
Besieged the Huntsman's Lodge
Local people interviewed.

Polly started early
On this her day off work.
He, exhausted, slept.
Like putting together
A large puzzle
Diligently she placed
Each piece in order.

"I'm sorry", he stirred
"You should have woken me..
The papers..?"
She had read them all,
Nothing he hadn't told her
Same old Press, nothing new.

"It reminds me of when
Guy was killed
Vultures fed 'til full
Under a flag convenient
'Our brave boys in Kabul'..
I think that this is better
There's hope in there somewhere,
Your country rejoices on TV
And wishes you were there."

"And if you feel you have to go
My feelings wouldn't end
You've never been The King to me
You're John, my love, my friend."

The King (15)

Galbraith appeared at 3pm
A meeting room in large Hotel
"I've men outside and on the door.
It's safe, it's just us here."

Several options open
But 'as you were' not one
Tensions in the village
Opinions split on what
Kathy Ridley had done.

Galbraith continued
Soft alliterative patter
"The truth, it appears, is out there now
For many, it won't matter,
As even today London wakes
To bullet and blood splatter,
A ship in trouble off the Gulf
Millions of gallons of crude
Yesterday's news you soon will be
I don't wish to seem rude."

"But we will need to close this box".

"Essentially, it's remain or return.
My sources tell me
In your country
They yearn for change of rule,
Hanker for the old days
Like old men speak at school.

And here too, you have people
Many to you not known
Who feel your pain and suffering
Say stay in peace, in this your home,,"

Inhaled, exhaled, and gazed through years
Let it all sink through.
King to thousands? Love to one
Saw Polly's blue and tearful eyes
And knew what should be done.

The King (16)

"And one more thing.."
Galbraith said lowly
"They want an interview
It might help…"

The following day, the same location
Galbraith, mob-handed, covert security,
Polly ushered into a bar.
They brought the TV big gun out
(We'll get some answers now).

"Before you ask me anything", John began.
"Let me tell you how this will work.
I've asked no fee, my own free will,
I will tell you my truth.
And if, indeed, I am a King
My word is not in question,
So respectfully sir you'll listen
Without need for interjection.
And I will afford you
Similar courtesy, when my story is done."

He looked around the small group
.."Or we can finish now.."

He told his tale
And in truth, there was not much to tell,
He was but a child,
Oblivious to worldly ways
To kingdoms and power
Lies and betrayal.
An innocent child,
Loved and adored
Never forsaken
Saved and spared
Through selfless act.

A good life led,
Improvement for all,
This final test, like calling gulls
Home was close to hand.

"What will you do now?"
The old hack asked
"A nation, it appears

Is calling home its son.
Do you consider this a duty
That now has to be done?"

John looked up
Polly, watching live feed
Looked down
Galbraith fidgeted
The old hack looked satisfied.

THE KING (17)

"I knew that you would ask me this.
And it is an excellent question
The only way true change will come
Is through a fair election.

It may be that I still have friends
But there are enemies too;
They are, of course, the reason
I sit here now, with you.

No doubt those rivals still exist
And will strive to prevent
A King is no solution
You can't replace, you reinvent.

No point for you to ask again
Next answer, as my last
How could I become their King
When 40 years have passed?

The monarchy died in the fire,
And with that, we are done;
Real change comes through a ballot box
Not through a King or gun.

The riches that your Old King held
Are kept for you, the Nation
And can be used to help re-build
With new administration.
My father's act of selflessness
Will never be forsaken
So I choose the one who held me up
When twice their world was shaken."

The King (18)

"Are we done?"
The men shook hands.
Galbraith glided, guided and
Like a phantom
Spirited the King away.

Downstairs, Polly waited
Heart fit to burst
Ran into his arms,
Gasping tears of pride and joy.

The interview was played in full
Across all the networks
Filling printed page and programme space
Candid smirks from the bourgeoisie
"Good on ya" from East End.

Great pressure built
In the old country;
Uncomfortable period
Outside interventions
Internal hostilities
All catalysts for change.

Then, when it came,
True to his word
The benefactor freed the funds
For hospitals, services and schools

And maybe it wouldn't
Be happy ever after
Although for John, this felt like closure
(As close as closure ever is).

And somewhere
In an English idyll,
The Reverend Peter Young
Conducted the marriage
Of Polly Read
To John, his beloved stepson.

And his wife Louise
Briefly took John aside
And softly she said unto him
"Here, at last
Is God."

The King (19)

A wooded lane
Near English beach,
Loving wife besides
This quiet man,
Now complete,
Moving lightly, as if dancing
Casting long evening shadows.

The trees have started budding
Gold breaks through the green
Over brook and under oak
Tells of life yet seen.

They gaze across the ocean
A thousand centuries wide
A photo from his wallet
Kissed, then placed inside.

A gentleman, polite and gracious,
A woman brave and kind
Long and loving happy days
All sadness left behind…

In this, their England.